CONTINUING   EDUCATION

IN

SENIOR CENTERS:

A HANDBOOK

By

Margaret Paul Joseph, Ph.D.

This book is dedicated

To everyone in

The Senior Center,

Town of Medfield, Massachusetts.

Thank you for being there!

CONTINUING EDUCATION IN SENIOR CENTERS:
A HANDBOOK

:

Contents

Introduction: The Why and the Wherefore

This little handbook is meant for Senior Centers everywhere. I have written it in the context of current discussions about the problems associated with aging and my fears that not enough is being done in our Centers to combat one of these problems: the scarcity of programs that energize the brain as it gets older. Anyone who knows anything about gerontology agrees that we need to challenge our mental faculties as we age. While some institutions try to remedy the situation by organizing such programs, Seniors themselves need to be made aware of the need for them and encouraged to enroll in them. The following pages are based on my experience in the local Senior Center where I decided to volunteer for this work after I retired. I was able to do so only because I was lucky enough to get the support of the Director who was (and is) enthusiastic and cooperative in helping me realize my ideas, The following pages outline what I learned from starting those programs. I hope they will be of use to Senior Centers anywhere in the world.

In Part I, the need for Senior Centers to organize such ventures in stimulating the brain are discussed. I point to various factors that have led to the deteriorating image of

Age as society has evolved and attitudes have changed. In ancient days, old people were respected and valued. Today, things are different and there has been a devaluation of the aged. Perhaps economics has contributed to this negative development.

In Part II, I offer a brief survey of the literature on geriatrics that has been written in recent years. I indicate the importance of local Senior Centers rather than places like university campuses for educational programs, and I maintain that it is only in Senior Centers that a whole population can be reached without attracting the charge of elitism. In this context, the importance of the Director of the Center is stressed. Without support from the top, programs such as these would languish. My argument is that structure is necessary; instead of permitting ad hoc happenings such as once a week card games, an afternoon of brain teasers or occasional talks about a variety of issues.

Part III, recommends various courses that would energize and involve Seniors rather than make them passive participants; and I suggest the methodology for conducting these courses. How is this focus on challenging the brain to be brought about? My answer is, by making use of anyone in the town, including other retirees, who are qualified and committed to serving their communities. Their expertise is a great way to keep their brains, too, pliant and healthy; and for both the teacher and the taught, expectations of a happy and healthy retirement will thus be satisfied.

I conclude by asserting that there are macro benefits to such programs that stimulate the brain: the burgeoning population of Senior Citizens all over the world could be encouraged by example of Senior Centers who are trail-blazers in this field. In this way, age will bring its own rewards in terms of enjoying a fulfilling life and better mental health.

A word about my choice of the e-book: I approached a publisher some months ago about this project but the Editor's initial enthusiasm about the idea of publishing for Senior Centers was dampened by those who did not think such a book would be marketable. This is understandable since marketability is of primary importance to bricks-and-mortar publishing houses, given the costs they incur and the limited budget within which Senior Centers operate. I then chose the e-book as a much easier format for them to purchase and, if necessary, print out. And since my goal is to help Seniors all over the world enjoy a happy old age, with the spread of the Internet it will be within the reach of anyone who wants to download it. My only aim is to turn the added years of our lives into years that are invigorating and therefore pleasant, healthy and fruitful. If this handbook succeeds in inspiring people in some small way, it will not have been in vain.

I would like to acknowledge the support I received from my family without whose help I might have stumbled in unfamiliar terrain. Their computer expertise turned my manuscript into the required e-book format.

My thanks also go to my friends in the Senior Center, Medfield, Massachusetts, for their active participation in my ideas for continuing education. My special thanks go to Roberta Lynch, Director, The Center at Medfield, Massachusetts: without her cooperation none of the programs described in the following pages would have been possible.

Part I

Analyzing the Why

i. *About Senior Centers:*

Senior Centers come in all shapes and sizes. Affluent towns that make good money from taxes build veritable Taj Mahals for their retirees. Towns with tight or minimal budgets find it hard to give them anything more than a room, sometimes squeezed into the basement of the Town Hall or a church, sometimes coaxed into the town's Parks and Recreation building, and sometimes non-existent as a physical location but dependent on the spirit of its old folks to meet, wherever. The Taj Mahal type boasts an abundance of facilities: exercise rooms fitted with the latest in fancy equipment; classrooms; a library; a computer room; a clinic complete with a part-time nurse; a dining room and attached state-of-the-art kitchen; a gift-shop; and a games room furnished with tables for playing cards or pool. The one-room Center on the other hand makes optimum use of its tiny space: dining tables become card tables after lunch, exercise is restricted to following physical fitness videos, gifts and books are crammed into one or two shelves, computers are installed near any

11

available outlet. But there is something both types have in common: Senior Citizens who have to be kept occupied or who learn to occupy themselves in various ways. So Bingo or Canasta flourish in some Centers, arts and crafts in another, computer use in a third... different ways of keeping busy for anyone who has reached what non-retirees like to call the Golden Years and what the Golden Folk themselves occasionally call the Boring Years.

Yes, old age can be boring. Much anticipated and longed for, retirement is peace and contentment for some and utter ennui for others. Gone is the soothing routine of organizing the children's lives, of worrying over a husband or wife, of cooking for the family. Or if the Senior Citizen was once in the workforce, gone now is the stress of commuting, of deadlines, of department meetings, of office politics. Gone too is the excitement of getting dressed for work, of planning constructive projects, of meeting interesting people, of water-cooler gossip, of socializing with folks from different departments. Now it is a question of grappling with the sudden loss of identity once bestowed by caring for a family or following a career, of self-esteem derived from doing a job that made a difference, whether in the home or in the office, and of the recognition or the salary that once brought the little luxuries of life.

Sometimes depression follows, merely from having nothing to do that seems worthwhile. Realization dawns that finally a certain stage has been reached in life's journey, the stage that is sometimes cruelly mocked in greeting cards. Entrenched negative attitudes suddenly blast into being, and Old Age sits and yawns in a corner, precipitously close to becoming the Club Bore with his interminable tales of past achievements. Or perhaps, becoming the Whiner Parent who imagines neglect from children and grandchildren and forgets that they have their own lives to lead. The evolution from Activity to Nothing-to do can result in Boredom.

I would like to suggest an alternative to this non-productive life. It is something that Senior Centers could undertake in order to make retirement as interesting as a career, with none of the career life's stresses and strains and with more of retirement's enjoyment and contentment. It is a magic formula that will combat those familiar and pernicious stereotypes about aging. It is also something that will reinforce its opposite: the determination not to worry about growing old, but to think instead that *now* there is the opportunity to enjoy oneself. We must remember that the psychology of positive thought keeps people mentally young at heart. As the saying goes, " Age is mind over matter and if you don't mind it doesn't matter." Is there a solution that is viable, besides being enjoyable? What is this magic formula?

It is an ingredient that is found, not in a bottle, but packed into a guidebook (such as this!) for Directors. It is called Continuing Education. It is something every Senior should plan on attempting for his or her own mental health and improved quality of life. Anyone connected with managing Senior Centers, whether its Directors or the government, must realize that investing in educational programs for retirees can turn into an advantage not just for retirees themselves but for the overall health of the community, the town and--in the macro context--the nation. "Age cannot wither nor custom stale her infinite variety," said Mark Anthony of Cleopatra, in Shakespeare's play. History tells us that the Egyptian queen never reached old age. But if she had, no doubt staying one step ahead of her enemies in Mediterranean politics would have helped to keep her brain cells alert and active.

Various famous people have commented on old age.

Thomas Jefferson said: "I see no comfort in . . . remaining a mere monument of the times which are past." What a depressing image of age is a monument! Cold and immovable, impressive but empty, a monument is a symbol of a life but not life itself. Instead of a monument, an anthill might be a better metaphor for old age: busy, interactive, highly structured. Abraham Lincoln's "And in the end, it's not the years in your life that count. It's the life in your years," is more appropriate. Unfortunately, old age today seems to be a synonym for decrepitude rather than dynamism.

Advancing age can be depressing, especially when a brutal mirror reflects grooves on the face and bags under the eyes. Of course, *everyone* gets old—even film-stars, some of whom might be unrecognizable if we saw them after a few decades. Female stars are not very visible once the unavoidable mantle of age drifts inexorably down over them. That's when it turns into a cloak of invisibility: they seem to disappear from the public eye. Only by checking the Internet and biography.com can we discover if they are still alive. Celebrity sightings are only those of the young and beautiful. But why should visibility worry us? Aging is a process that happens to everyone, after all—that is, if they are lucky! What is important is *healthy* aging.

ii. *In ages past*:

In his History of Old Age, Georges Minois claims that up to the Middle Ages old people were considered a gerontocracy, so powerful were they. Perhaps this was due to the fact that mortality rates were high, so anyone who lived to old age was honored and respected and had a role in society. People might have thought that a long life was the sign of favor from the gods. Old people held positions of authority. The word "Senator" can be traced back to the days of the Romans when the Senate was a gathering of old men. In ancient Sparta, those in charge of government were called "elders." In Asia, the respect paid to old men ensured that they remained a vital part of the household till death. There was no thought of relegating them to old age homes. The logic seems to have been that if they lived so long, they had to be respected for that achievement. Whatever the reason, in centuries past it seems as if old people had a certain power.

If this is true and the old were valued in medieval times, what has changed now? Why have they lost power over the years? One reason, says Minois, may be due to the development of printing. Before that, oral history was the norm. Old people told tales and young folks listened. They learned about their family's past or about their country's history from the lips of a grandfather or grandmother who thus became a symbol of continuity. But today, *the book* has obviated the need for turning with respect to such sources. Why listen to people whose memories, after all, may not be all that reliable? Why not turn to the (supposed) authority of the printed page? So the power of the written word has replaced the power of the oral tradition. The book has assumed precedence over the voice.

Is it a fact that in medieval times there was a respected gerontocracy? Is this something we imagine or was it a reality? Minois admits that perhaps what research shows is the importance paid to a minority of learned or affluent or aristocratic old men and women, not the ordinary majority who, perhaps, were not particularly respected. Before the dawn of the Middle Ages, the Greeks apparently valued beauty so highly that old people might have been treated with contempt because they were no longer handsome or beautiful. We have no way of knowing if this applied to all sections of the population or not, and obviously this was not always the case. Alexander the Great chose leaders according to merit, not according to age or appearance. Plato idealized old age in his works, though Aristotle seems to have been more negative. In Roman times, Cicero gave us his views on old age through the mouths of two characters, and they are very positive.

He claimed that his writing was one way in which he kept his brain alert. He was "an active student of Greek literature; and to keep my memory in training" he says, "I adopt the practice of [running] over in my mind all that I have heard and said and done during the day. That is my intellectual exercise, my running-track of the brain—and while I sweat and toil at the task I do not greatly miss my bodily strength…. For the man whose whole life consists of study and activity of this kind does not notice old age creeping up on him. Instead, he grows old by slow stages, imperceptibly…" (Cicero, p. 228). If Cicero could keep busy in old age all those centuries ago, why should we not do so now, in our (supposedly) more advanced century, instead of finding that the opposite holds true?

iii. *Changes in attitude:*

There are reasons for the change in attitude to the old today and perhaps it all began with the societal changes of urbanization and industrialism, twin engines of a certain kind of devaluation. With the rise of industrialism in the eighteenth century, the economic balance began to shift from the rural to urban. Urbanization removed sons from villages where the family had once lived together. The newly nuclear family became so absorbed in making ends meet that old parents who did not have the skills to make a living for themselves in the city were often left behind, literally or psychologically. Sometimes they stayed on in the villages where they had lived all their lives. If they joined their children in the town, they were perhaps left in corners where they gave the least trouble. Industrialization led to commercialization of life and this in turn led to the downgrading of the generation that was not a contributing factor to economic prosperity because it did not earn a living and it did not succeed at commerce. In other words, it was a generation that did not make money. In the final analysis, loss of earning capacity meant loss of power. Old folks no longer have the power of "pelf" so they have become the reverse of a gerontocracy.

"Retirement" was an unknown word centuries ago. People worked as long as they had the health to do so, and after that their children looked after them. Today retirement, at least in the Western world, means having the capability to live independently because pensions and social security provide the basics without old parents having to depend on their children. But retirement does not earn enough to instigate the commercial world into focusing on the needs of the retired. Senior Citizens are not big spenders, so why worry about making products for them? As a result, manufacturers cater to the needs of babies, children, teenagers and young couples, whose purchases fill their coffers and delight Wall Street. Fashion houses do not design clothes for the over-sixties for the simple reason that it is not worth their money. The same applies to other areas of business. Contrast the buying power of working parents and that of retired grandparents and the economic reason for what is being called "ageism" becomes clear. Contrast the sales figures from products for the frenetic teenage shopper with sales figures for the apologetic and undemanding Senior, and ageism becomes even more clear. Contrast the amounts that couples spend on their children to what they spend on their own parents. Look at the only manufacturers who seem to make money on Seniors—for obvious reasons, they are pharmaceutical companies. Hence the reluctance of Big Business to spend money on old people and their needs, unless those needs feed back into the financial system that boosts their profits.

iv. *Economics and Aging:*

The importance of money in the context of retirement is proved by a global study done in 2004 by the HSBC bank. Surveying 11,453 adults living in four continents and spread over ten countries, their project was called "The Future of Retirement" and is an important indication of differing attitudes all over the world. Not surprisingly, in economically poorer countries like China, India and Mexico, the stress was on family and the belief that children would take care of old parents—though that may now be changing. In Britain, Canada, France, Japan and the United States, the attitude is to depend on oneself and to a certain extent on the government, and includes plans for remaining active as long as possible. The study was part of a project undertaken by Age Wave, a firm founded by Ken Dychtwald. Dychtwald's firm tries to anticipate products and services that companies can provide for older adults and the Boomer generation so that they can lead more productive lives. This is again a sign of how in current thinking retirement plans are synonymous with money. He directed the attention of Fortune 500 companies to this idea. The Dychtwald theory is that certain industries should be guided to profit from the retirement demographics that are beginning to burgeon. This would be the start of increasing attention being paid to retirees because they help various companies—for example those who specialize in financial services, health products, leisure and entertainment, and so on. The financial health of the providers will perhaps parallel the emotional and mental and physical health of the Senior. But unfortunately, Dychtwald mentions education for the ordinary Senior only in passing. It does not seem to be a major component of his concern for improvement in life-styles.

The label Age Wave somehow carries connotations of affluent Seniors, of gray-haired but energetic men and women surfing the waves, full of vigor and enthusiasm. This picture has little to do with that brought to mind by Helpage, another organization that focuses on the old, but a very different category of old: those who are at the bottom of the economic ladder. Established in 1983, Helpage does what its name implies. It helps the aged in deprived areas in parts of the Americas, Asia and Africa. It trains members to support government and non-government bodies that provide care and develop programs for the aged. Helpage conducted its own survey, and found that in 1950, 8 out of every 100 people were over 60 years old. By 2050, 22 out of every 100 people will be over 60 and, because of population figures, most of them will be in poor countries. This indicates the urgent need for education so that they can cope with the problems of aging. Through the learning process, people find solutions. But solutions vary, just as demands vary, according to the demographics of age in each country. And demographics tell their own story.

It is an unfortunate fact that in the West youth seems to be valued more than age, unlike Eastern societies where tradition mandates that age be respected and youth subordinated to parental control. Wealthier countries may not need the kind of education that enables people to overcome ill health and poverty, issues that burden old Africans, for example. Africa has to face challenges from HIV and other diseases, from malnutrition, from lack of pension plans or government-sponsored security in old age. These challenges are met with greater success in wealthier nations. Presumably an old person in North America is more educated about HIV than one in Africa. Since that is the case, the learning paradigm in rich countries should be a different kind, with a different focus. It should be the kind that engages the individual in exercising the brain by learning something new, not something he or she already knows. This paradigm is called Continuing Education.

Part II

Solutions to the Wherefore

i. *Research on Aging:*

The point I wish to make is that Continuing Education is a vital component in the mental as well as physical health of our Seniors. It need not and should not have anything to do with Big Business. Instead, it should have everything to do with Senior Centers. Why? Because in a functioning democracy, *every Senior, not just those who have the money,* should be able to tap into resources that will strengthen their mental capacities. This means those Seniors who are on a fixed income and cannot afford the high-flying life-style in retirement that more affluent retirees can enjoy. These are the Seniors who gravitate to Senior Centers; and they constitute the majority of the older population. Surely life should not be measured only in terms of commerce!

Rebecca Gardyn's article "Retirement Redefined," published in 2000, cites the change in the number of retirees who used to lead sedentary lives. From 34% of the men in 1985, it morphed to 28% ten years later. Among women the percentages slipped too. Instead of the 44 % who led sedentary lives in 1985, ten years later it was 39%, according to the article. Obviously retirees are becoming more active and this, the author points out, presents an "incredible marketing opportunity." According to her statistics, by 2030 there will be 70 million people in the United States, or 20% of the population, ready to retire. They will have better health, more money, and more time than those who went before them. Programs have to be established to serve them so they can grow old in the most fulfilling manner. And fulfillment need not necessarily be linked only to commercial products or programs. There are other ways in which to be productive.

Several important studies have encouraged us to consider the various ways in which the process of aging can be tackled successfully. In *Vital involvements in old age* (1986) Erik Erikson divides the process of human development into stages from youth to old age. Old Age, he says, is a time when productivity is important because it brings fulfillment. Everyone needs some sort of challenge. Challenge results in the creativity that responds to the challenge; and creativity in turn results in satisfaction.

Rowe and Kahn's *Successful Aging* (1998) discusses what the authors call "new gerontology." Aging does not mean withering, to use the Cleopatra reference again. Healthy eating, exercise, vitamins, lifestyle and attitude are all as important as genes in deciding how one ages. Myths about the aged have to be demolished, myths that make for ageism, wrong beliefs about old people that are as much a matter of prejudice and injustice as racism or sexism. The authors acknowledge that the process by which information is processed slows as we get older, but "the more you have, the more you do…the more you preserve." (p.182). Most importantly, they tout education as the strongest foundation for maintaining "high cognitive function." Self esteem and performance act on each other and mental faculties can improve with age. But while they stress the need for creativity and social interaction, their study is not about the means of achieving them. They do not get down to the nuts and bolts of establishing programs.

Ken Dychtwald's *Age Power: how the 21st century will be ruled by the new old* (1999) mentions the different types of activities, both related to work and to leisure, that enable Seniors to "master a new skill, craft, or field of knowledge by becoming private students of talented individuals" (p.74). He coins the word "individuation," meaning the beginning of a new interest in an older adult's life. However he too does not specify any study programs by which this can be accomplished since it is outside the scope of his focus.

In the same way, *Aging Without Growing Old* (2000) by Judy and Laura McFarland, has more to say about the admittedly serious need for proper nutrition than about nourishing the brain with new ideas. Not that vitamins, alternative medicine or other physical elements are not essential to aging: they are. But they do not comprise the whole story. Mental as well as physical nutrition is vital for complete health.

Gene Cohen thesis is similar, but with a slight difference, in *The Creative Age: Awakening human potential in the 2nd half of life* (2000). There are different forms of creativity in people, he opines, but what is necessary is to realize that it is possible to encourage it, to recognize its importance and work to develop its growth. In this way we can "change our lives as we age" (p.301). Unlike the rest of our body cells, it is proved that brain cells can grow. This is a scientific discovery of tremendous import. It means that even if physical health declines, mental health does not have to. Neuroscience has proved that with "mental exercise" the brain can not just grow, but even change as it grows.

Thomas Perls describes how "dendrites" can be grown by existing cells in the brain. These help to overcome brain damage and research has shown that they can actually be stimulated by learning new skills, taking up new activities or doing some other kind of "brain-training." The more the brain is used, the more does it regenerate itself and the more can fulfillment be derived from living. Active use of the brain can trigger "neurogenesis" or the growth of new brain cells as well as "arborization—the forming of connections between them." (Schneider, p.193).

David Snowden's *Aging with Grace* (2001), also called *The Nun Study*, is another example of a book that discusses the need for mental activity in aging people. Such activity may prevent or delay the onset of age-related diseases like Alzheimer's. He tells us about two nuns whose cases he studied in his research on the subject. One got her Ph.D. in her 50s, studied computers in her 70s, and went to Africa to work in the missions. The other worked in the sewing room, had no mental activity, and developed Alzheimers (pp. 78-79). This is an interesting case study, even if it is not conclusive.

Dr. Victoroff's *Saving Your Brain* (2002) is an important contribution to our understanding of how our brains work, and what can be done to "*Boost Brain power, Improve memory and Protect yourself against Aging and Alzheimer's,*" as he claims in his sub-title. There are enlightening chapters on stress, jobs, sex and diet in connection with the brain. In chapter 18, entitled "Brain Fitness II: Using Your Mind to Build Your Brain," Dr. Victoroff repeats what *The Nun Study* postulated: the relation between using the brain and losing it, or in other words, the fact that the possibility of developing Alzheimer's disease is much less when the brain is used for learning something new. He cites proof of this from various studies conducted by prestigious research teams and adds that "pursuing a cognitively demanding occupation through adulthood seems to protect against memory loss," and he mentions a Swedish study that indicated the connection between manual labor and the risk of Alzheimer's in comparison to more mentally stimulating jobs..." (p. 367). All that seems to be necessary is an ordinary education and some kind of mental challenge. The brain changes all the time. What we could do when we were younger may be difficult with age. But on the other hand, what we do when we are older, we may not have been able to do in youth. So since cells keep changing, dying in some parts, regenerating themselves in others, it is important to keep stimulating our thinking powers since "exposure to cognitive challenges builds up the brain." (p. 376). Like Perls, he links the increase of dendrites to brain activity. So he encourages older people to live life to the fullest, to study, teach, learn a new instrument, and so on. "Exploring with our minds delights our brains," he concludes (p. 384).

George Vaillant's groundbreaking book *Aging Well: surprising guideposts to a happier life* (2002) is again important in what it sets out to do: show the results of evaluations done over a number of years on chosen sectors of the population, and the conclusions based on these studies. All point to the necessity for healthy attitudes when aging. He coins a new word: "generativity," or the giving of oneself to the community, something that volunteers do all the time. Vaillant pins it all down to four activities that could make the life of a Senior rewarding: the old network of colleagues at work should now be replaced by a new network of retirees. They may rediscover pastimes for which they had no time before: golf, gardening or card games, or creative outlets such as writing or painting. Or they could summon up the courage to learn something entirely new. Thus Seniors achieve the four C's, he says: contentment, compensation, competence and commitment. Vaillant's anecdote about the woman who graduated from Harvard at the age of eighty-nine is inspiring, and it is exactly the point that I wish to make:

that learning is a vital factor in achieving the four C's, and as a result, in growing old in the best possible way. The fact that the conclusions drawn by the authors of all these books are now taken for granted only shows how their studies have contributed to our present knowledge of gerontology. "Healthy aging," "successful aging," or "positive aging" have now become buzzwords in the field.

A recent study (2004) entitled "The Relation Between Brain Activity During Memory Tasks and Years of Education in Young and Older adults," (*Neuropsychology*, 2005, Vol. 19, No. 2) was conducted by a group of scientists from the University of Toronto: Mellanie V. Springer, MSc., Anthony R. McIntosh, PhD., Gordon Winocur, PhD., and Cheryl L. Grady, PhD. Since forgetfulness is, after all, one of the aspects of getting old, the researchers used a memory task to test older adults   To their immense interest it was found that Alzheimer's disease was less damaging in those who had more education than in others. They researched the brain activity of 14 adults between the ages of 18 to 30 who had 11 to 20 years of education, and 19 adults aged 65 or more who had 8 to 21 years of education. Their method was to give the participants several memory workouts, at the same time doing MRIs to examine the brain. They found that "education was positively co-related with frontal activity" in the brain of the older people, but that it was the opposite for younger adults. The reason still does not seem to be clear, but may perhaps be attributed to the fact that highly educated Seniors used more of the "frontal cortex," and that helped cognition. In other words, brain work.

. It all boils down to fulfillment, which in turn boils down to self-confidence and mental health. Motivation is a key factor. A re-reading of Maslow and his classic essay of a few decades ago, "The Theory of Motivation" will sustain this point. He lists the "needs" experienced by human beings. One need is the need for self-actualization. Anything based on achievement increases our feelings of self-respect and results in self-confidence because we know we have gained recognition and are appreciated by others. Without these feelings we degenerate into inferiority, weakness and neuroticism.

My argument is that this theory can be applied to older adults. Self-actualization can be realized through learning new skills. Whether through music, painting, woodcarving, astronomy or whatever, self-actualization can result in the physical and mental health that makes old age enjoyable and sustainable.

Apart from serious studies on healthy aging, there are more "popular" books on the same subject. These do not claim to be analytical or scientific. They are easy to read and more personal in their approach to getting old, anecdotes from the author's life being a common feature. While such anecdotes make interesting reading they sometimes have the opposite effect from what they intend to do. Women (and it is usually women who write such books) overcome odds such as widowhood or divorce, and rewrite their lives, whether by taking up new interests or turning to new careers. This is admirable. But to some readers (again, mainly women) the spirit of enterprise, the gritty determination, the sheer pluck that goes into renewing their lives can be intimidating. It is easy for some readers to say to themselves: "If she can do that, so can I!" And it is equally easy for other readers to say to themselves: "Well, she might be able to do such and such, but that's beyond me!" And these go back to their own problems, feeling even more depressed. Such anecdotal and popular books are Gail Sheehy's *New Passages: mapping your life across time* (1995), Frances Weaver's *The Girls with the Grandmother Faces* (1996), and Abigail Trafford's *My Time: making the most of the rest of your life* (2004). They all include the same ideas that are seen in the more scholarly books: the need for new areas of learning, the toxic myths about the negative aspects of aging, the quality of life during Seniorhood, and the scientifically proven advantages of education

Just as using a muscle increases its strength, using the brain builds it up. Brain workouts boost mental prowess, says an article in *Consumer Reports* (October 2004). Various types of workouts are suggested—memorizing poems, playing chess or bridge, joining book clubs, doing jigsaw puzzles, solving crosswords—but all point to this one fact: mental stimulation from leisure activities is all-important. There is a caveat here, however: this kind of brain work can sometimes become routine and may not stimulate neuro-plasticity, or the growth of new cells, as much as new tasks can. An article by Sharon Begley in the Wall Street Journal's Science pages warns that "operating on autopilot doesn't help. Only mental tasks that you focus on intently can produce the physical changes that let old neurons learn new tricks." These days, the brain's zoning map—with different neighborhoods assigned different functions—is looking as malleable as putty. Evidence of this "plasticity" has been piling up for more than a decade, but now neuroscientists are realizing that it is more radical than they thought, and that it lasts well into adulthood.

There is so much talk in the media, and not just among Seniors, about the obligation to exercise, exercise, exercise, in order to stay healthy. But apart from games of different kinds how many opportunities are there for Seniors to *exercise the mind*? Why are they not encouraged to exercise that particular part of themselves? Why the focus only on trips, on eating out, on knitting? All enjoyable ways of passing time, without a doubt, but surely there are other avenues of enjoyment, interests that can attract those who would like to use their minds? The survey of literature on the subject (given above) shows its importance. More research is needed and more is being done, but we do not have to wait for scholarly conclusions to be published. There has to be a way to increase those little gray cells that keep us alert, involved and curious. And that points to the need for a structured learning environment that is accessible to *all* older adults. Hence the goal of energizing Senior Centers--though it must also be noted in passing, that there are other organizations that would benefit as well.

For example, patients in nursing homes, assisted living homes and rehabilitation centers would profit, too, from educational programs. To those who are mentally alert it is a boon to have someone keep their minds off their illnesses by having them learn something new.

Educational Activity Programs for Older Adults by Williams and Downs is a strong contribution in this field and is replete with ideas that could be used among older patients. Like healthy, mobile Seniors, this group too needs self-respect and respect from others, say the two authors. "Self-actualization" is achieved through developing "one's full potential in areas of self-development, creativity, and self expression." (p.6). Self-esteem is an important component of mental health, but especially for an aging group of people who have opted (out of choice or necessity) for quieter lifestyles instead of full-fledged careers. The self-esteem that goes with producing some kind of output is necessary for self-validation; and homebound Seniors need it as much as, or perhaps more than any in Senior Centers. This advice, connected with the proper motivation, is worth applying to any group of Seniors. .

ii. *Senior Citizens and the College Campus:*

While the importance of what Vaillant calls 'creativity' and 'generativity' are acknowledged, the writers mentioned above have not specified actual classes that Senior Centers could start for their members. There are Public Libraries that sometimes have literacy courses for non-English speaking Seniors. But what about regular college type courses? In Europe, a graceful new phrase was framed for Seniors who want to continue studying after retirement: "Third Age." This is the period of retirement that follows an adult's career life. In the United States it is sometimes (optimistically) called the Golden Years. Classes are conducted under the auspices of what began in Europe as the University of the Third Age and what is now very active in many countries. Finland has an impressive program, as Joseph Yenerall tells us in his article "Educating an aging Society: The University of the Third Age in Finland."

In the United States, classes linked to "U3A" as it is called are held, but again most of them are linked to universities or community colleges, not to Senior Centers. Massachusetts, for example, has several ongoing programs in locations ranging from the Cape Cod Community College to Harvard University. More than three hundred continuing education programs exist all over the country. Road Scholar: Adventures in Lifelong Learning (which used to be called Elderhostel), Learning in Retirement, the University of the Third Age, among others—all offer a wide range of courses.

All of them are linked to academic settings, are taught by either peers or professors and are available to any interested Senior. Institutes of Learning in Retirement, Lifelong Learning Centers and other academic programs offer courses for audit or full participation at a nominal fee. The University of Connecticut conducts courses for Seniors in its Institute for Learning in Retirement. Another organization is The Lifelong Learners Institute which has a wide-ranging smorgasbord of courses.

The American Council on Education published reports on seniors and continued learning. Titled "Mapping New Directions; Higher Education for Older Adults" (2008), the final study was on "Reinvesting in the Third Age: Older Adults and Higher Education." Their findings, based on focus groups and a national survey, researched the analysis of forty-two percent of institutions in the United States that responded to the survey. It proved that only ten percent of the older adult population took advantage of courses offered by these institutions. One of the interesting comments was that perhaps the terminology could be changed, an idea that several seniors themselves endorse. For example, instead of calling older adults "seniors," they could be called "lifelong learners" or "the third age." The word "seniors" seems to carry connotations of impoverished senility, to put it harshly.

One factor that stymies efforts to involve older adults in continuing education may be because all these programs are conducted at college campuses. Then there is the cost angle. Some of these institutes require an annual fee of $25/ to $30/ in addition to a course fee of $15/. One website listed the computer course at $25/- while the financial course (investment strategies, etc.) cost much more. Marketability seems to be the key factor in deciding the level of fees. Road Scholar has a huge variety of courses for older adults, most of which are linked to travel plus learning. The charges are reasonable but everyone may not want to spend money traveling in order to learn. Most Seniors travel to experience the relaxed enjoyment derived from sight-seeing, entertainment and restaurants rather than education. Some institutions conduct programs online. All courses are conducted with different aims in mind and all seem to be doing very well. But this is not enough. Should not such courses be available to *all* Seniors? Should profit and commercial concerns be the norm even after retirement? Unfortunately, college courses do not meet everyone's requirements.

The majority of Seniors avoid learning in academic environments for the following reasons: a) they do not live close enough to a campus to make driving there practical;

b) they do not want to drive at night—many classes are conducted after dark; c) they are intimidated by the physical setting of the college campus; d) they do not have the confidence to join a classroom full of young people; e) while many colleges offer free classes, all do not—Seniors may not want to spend money on tuition, even if rates are reduced. Instead of the campus type of physical location, there is instead a vital need for Senior Centers to focus on providing such services to older adults. These centers are accessible to all and pose no psychological threat. Most Seniors might prefer its cozier surroundings since there is a more relaxed and casual ambiance and an atmosphere of "we're all on the same page. " While the programs in academia are open to any and everyone, it usually happens that taking the whole Senior population into account, only a minority find their way to them.

Thus, without meaning to be so, such programs become elitist. In a functioning democracy, programs for older adults should never smack of elitism. Though the next few years will see a huge crowd of college graduates enter the Senior population, too many of today's Seniors have never stepped into a college campus in their lives. It is a moot point if they can be coaxed into doing so after the age of fifty. If not there, where could they find mental stimulation? When they look to their Senior Centers there are no such programs. Instead, Senior Centers tend to focus more on the physical side of aging, on health issues and visits from the VNA, on Meals on Wheels and subsidized lunches, with little in the way of programs that would benefit those who are interested in learning something that will stimulate the mind. This focus on frailty in elders has the negative side-effect of reinforcing that dangerous stereotype of old age: the inexorable and unavoidable decline into decrepitude.

It is true that such programs are offered elsewhere, as previously mentioned. But there are problems with other programs. Apart from the money involved in high tuition fees, where are they to find courses for which they can sign up? Online courses mandate the possession of computers and the knowledge to navigate the internet. Seniors do possess computers, but they still form a minority. Most Senior Centers now have computers and this is a better social setting, but where studying new material is concerned, it may not be ideal.

The National Institute of Senior Centers would do well to investigate the many ways in which older adults can achieve satisfaction from more programs than are now available in Centers. Unfortunately, issues of health and nutrition take up a good bit of time and money. Politics within institutes could be an obstacle too. It is not easy to get funding because, as we have seen, there is a type of discrimination against the aged, and this deflects public funds towards a younger population. Constant battles are waged in town halls between the two age groups that represent the two sides: parents who want money given to the schools where their children study, and Seniors who grumble at the higher property taxes involved and the diversion of funds from their own needs. There are no plans for, and there is little interest in spending money on establishing structured educational programs for older adults. Neither the website of the National Institute of Aging nor the National Institute of Senior Centers make reference to such programs. By 2015 there will be a huge increase in the Senior population. We need to anticipate it now.

I suggest that with better health, longer lives, earlier retirement, and a fast approaching Boomer-turned-Senior generation it is time for Senior Centers—and there are approximately 10 to 12000 Centers in the country—to focus not just on Meals on Wheels, health clinics, entertainment ideas or trips. If they do not answer to the changing needs of Seniors they will find themselves filled with increasing crowds of the senile old. They would have lost the opportunity to turn their populations into mentally as well as physically active contributors to society. They would have defeated the very reason for their existence. So it is time to get down to specifics and establish such programs in Senior Centers, it is time for them to discourage ageism and encourage self-esteem and empowerment through education, it is time to focus on use-it-or-lose-it ideas that will help Seniors turn the inevitable process of aging into something stimulating.

iii. *Role of the Director:*

There is one aspect of service to the aging that has to be noted: the Directors themselves need to have vision and motivation. Too often they are focused more on the usual activities mentioned above: meals, health, entertainment and so on. There is no doubt that there are obstacles: space in which to conduct classes, people to teach classes, money to run the classes, or Seniors who are not interested in classes. Directors often profess helplessness in stretching the budget to encompass such programs, they cite town indifference, logistical problems, or difficulties with the mechanics of managing classes. It is quite a list. But the Director worth her salt will try to push the idea of *learning* as an activity that is of primary importance to the mental, emotional and physical health of Seniors. This is an aspect of aging that is still to take root in most Directors' minds. Nothing is impossible to those who are properly motivated. He/she should never give the excuse that such programs cannot be established. They can. They must.

Directors must also remember one of the first principles of good management: that since volunteers work without remuneration, it is mandatory that their work be recognized. It should be made clear to the Seniors citizens with whom volunteers interact that they are motivated by a spirit of service and dedication to the community, and that monetary gain is not involved. A bouquet of flowers or a box of candy awarded on Volunteer Recognition Day goes a long way to validate their efforts to help. So do little notes of thanks from those whom they do help. Since volunteers are human, it is savvy management when the Director demonstrates, in more than just words, that they are valuable to the Center. This makes them feel rewarded by the community.

Social interconnectedness is one of the advantages of attending a Senior Center. Churches provide this atmosphere of collegiality among Seniors since, in many places, going to church is one way of staying connected with the community. But church attendance seems to be declining; so it is possible to envisage a time when the Boomer generation will require other venues where they can meet and greet people. The Senior Center is the obvious answer. Not just through Bridge or Bingo, but in a classroom atmosphere they could connect even more deeply. Interaction is vital for mental health and, as a corollary, of physical health. Must not the Director, then, try and encourage it? It has been proved that this kind of social connectedness makes for longer and healthier lives. Isolation and loneliness, on the other hand, trigger depression, memory loss and ultimately, possible dementia.

Another reason why Directors should provide learning programs is that in a democracy all strata of society should be given the opportunity to progress. As mentioned above, college and university campuses are not as easy to adjust to as the Senior Center. It is the duty of the Director, then, as a means of putting the mission statement into action, to help the lower income groups of Seniors. These, in fact, are the ones who would most benefit by learning programs. Not only does the mind become energized through mental stimulation, but they are inspired to educate themselves about all kinds of social issues.

Until now economically deprived Seniors may not have had either the opportunity or the funds to attend college level classes. Why should not the Director encourage them to dip their toes into the ocean of knowledge? Senior Centers had better not ignore possibilities for progress. If they did, they would fail in their mission of discovering the needs of Seniors and planning programs that will meet those needs.

One way of doing so is for the staff in Senior Centers to remind Seniors of the freedom they now enjoy from the worries and responsibilities of bringing up children, working from nine to five, caring for spouses, and other burdens that younger people have to bear. Why not make use of their new freedom and search for those talents, that creativity that has been buried so long. That is the way to move forward instead of jogging in the same spot, without inspiration, without motivation, without fulfillment. A short talk on the medical aspects of aging and the therapeutic advantages of learning might be helpful. Seniors are interested in anything that has to do with their health. If the Director combined an ice-cream social with a pep-talk on registering for classes, and embroidered the talk with a chart that showed how the brain gets strengthened with mental activity, it might have encouraging results.

iv. Expectations in Retirement:

What do Seniors want from retirement? The Lehrer News Hour telecast on 12/1/05 discussed the Science of Aging with David Sinclair, a doctor from Harvard Medical School. He explained how molecular biology may extend humans' lifespan. Experiments had shown, he said, that laboratory animals on calorie-restricted diets live longer. Rodents, for example, lived longer on restricted diets than those on regular ones. It seems as if genes are the controlling factor. Perhaps, said Dr. Sinclair, anti-aging genes may have developed millions of years ago at a time when there was not enough to eat. These genes created a "cellular emergency response" in order to survive. So the questions could be asked: could these genes be turned on even without a restricted diet? But this raises the question: if age can be extended, how is it going to be spent? Baby boomer surveys show that this new generation of soon-to-Seniors is going to be very different from today's Seniors.

Boomers are better educated than their parents, have better health, and are more interested in continuing to work—though most of them want to work part-time. The falling birthrate will ensure that jobs will still be available because there are going to be fewer younger people to fill them. Many will want to venture into new paths instead of jogging along the same career track they followed before retirement. Training will be welcomed, new knowledge will be enjoyed, education will be the way to go. Instead of looking back at the stereotypical picture of what older people have been doing till now--games, golf or gambling--it is time to start thinking outside the box. New directions with new perspectives are imperative. Only fresh thinking will prepare us for the different Retired Life scenario the future will bring, rather than the scenario that prevails today. Reality checks should egg Seniors into action plans that fulfill what they envisage as happy, not bored, retirement.

According to the survey mentioned earlier, Canada scored highest in the quality of Seniors' expectations of retirement. The United States and Japan were ranked second and third respectively. Developing countries scored the least. Here, as in other parts of the world, people are living longer but with no plans as to how to spend their bonus years. In developing countries, social services are limited partly from financial constraints and partly because it is assumed, as mentioned above, that the old are looked after by their children. China's Confucian tradition mandated it. So does India's Hindu principle of dharma or right behavior. In Africa, the younger population will continue to hold its own, but this is the poorest continent in the world. The breakup of the African joint family, the migration of younger people, and the gradually changing focus from the community to the individual, are all corroding ancient practices. And something has to fill its place. Instead of having huge global populations suffering from senile dementia or Alzheimer's—and this would affect the whole global economy—should we not rather have millions of older adults who, by using their brains, now have far better mental health than they ever had before?

Unfortunately, little is being done to help structure programs in poorer countries. "Old Age Tsunami" by Nicholas Eberstadt points to dropping birthrates and rising Senior populations (WSJ.com, November 15, 2005). In Russia, public health has deteriorated and life expectancy for men is lower than India's as of now. How can pensioners depend on the support of poorly paid workers to subsidize them? In India, birthrates in the South are dropping too (the North has a younger median age) and the graying population is rising without the income level to sustain it. China is the worst off in this regard. According to Eberstadt, between 2005 and 2025, "about two-thirds of China's total population growth will occur in the 65-plus ages" and this may amount to about 200 million people trying to subsist in what is still a poor society, with most of this number uneducated. The point of his article is that this situation cannot be considered a local problem. It is a global issue since today what happens to markets in one part of the world affects the other. "Will the aging of the Third World have unanticipated spillover effects for the world economy?" asks the writer. No one is sure. What is sure, however, is that developing countries by and large imitate developed economies. In time they will also have the same expectations regarding their retirement.

The United States exports its democratic ideas to the rest of the world: its music, films, fashions and even fast food chains. It should now export its ideas on rejuvenating huge numbers of older adults and in this way benefit the whole world. It can continue to be a leader in this enormously vital area of all-round care for older people. After so many centuries, should we not claim more progress compared to the ancient people who lived long ago? What is the use of our vibrant economies, state of the art technology, and advanced healthcare if our old people are not better off psychologically and mentally than their ancestors? Should we not try and reach an approximation of the ideal as envisaged by the great men of Greece and

Rome who analyzed the benefits of living to a great age? If we do not, we have made no real progress at all towards happiness and contentment. We have not maximized our potential and achieved self-fulfillment. There has been no transcendence. What is the point in living forever without using our brains to their optimum capacity? A long life without learning, creativity and fulfillment would be to live like the Struldbrugs, the mythical race that Swift writes about in "Gulliver's Travels."

On one of his voyages, Gulliver meets the Struldbrugs and is fascinated to discover that they never die. In that case, thinks Gulliver, they must have met all those famous people from centuries past, whom we only read about. Delighted that he could now talk about them with these men and women who had achieved immortality on earth, Gulliver tries to converse with them. To his horror and disgust he realizes that they cannot remember anything of the past. All they have is life without memory, understanding or will. They might as well be dead.

Imagine having to cope with a population that is decrepit rather than dynamic! Demographic statistics show that in future old people are going to outnumber the young in many developed countries. Do we want this to happen to all of them? Instead of doing nothing to prevent that horror, Senior Centers have the power to avoid this type of mental sterility. It would be a tragedy of Brobdinagian proportions if Directors of Senior Centers did not seize the opportunity to do so.

Part III

Class Models for Courses

i. *Getting Started*:

How does one begin Continuing Education programs for Seniors? What are the nuts and bolts that have to be engineered into place?

It might be useful to describe the way in which our local Center started such classes. Once I thought that Continuing Education would benefit Seniors I decided to tout the plan to the Director. Did she think it would be a good idea? What would the response be? Would it infringe on other programs? Would it be considered too elite or exclusive?

No, was her answer to all these questions. But what would be taught, she asked. The subjects, I suggested, would depend on whether we could find volunteers with qualifications. The hour of day when classes could be held would have to be decided since we would have to find a place to conduct the class and certain rooms might not be free. What did she think? To start things off, I offered to teach a course in English Literature,.

She was delighted; but she had more questions and these were more specific.

Did I have the qualifications to teach a course? (Yes. I have a Ph.D. in English Literature). Would I need remuneration? (No, this would be volunteer work. Besides, I knew that the Center was strapped for funds). How often would the class meet? (Once a week at a convenient time for everybody, taking into account the fact that the Seniors' Bus would be needed to pick up those who did not drive). Where would we meet? (If the Public Library was willing, we could use their Conference Room if we did not have a free room in our Center). Would there be any fees? (Yes, there would be a registration fee that would go towards the expenses of photocopying materials, etc). Another reason for the fee is that once payment is involved, Seniors feel more committed to the program and less likely to be complaisant about missing sessions. (The actual fee would vary according to the economic level of the town). Could I advertise the project by writing it up in order to inform the community of our new enterprise? I willingly agreed to do so.

So I wrote a paragraph about the new program that the Senior Center was going to introduce. It was a short paragraph and appeared in the newsletter that is mailed to Seniors, that is displayed in the Public Library, and that is kept in the Center for anyone to pick up. Living as we do near Boston, I had chosen an area of interest to New Englanders—New England Poets—and wrote it up as enticingly as I could. Considering we are in a state that is so rich in famous literary figures, would it not be fun to read about them? The same paragraph appeared in two consecutive issues of our town's newspaper, and I specifically requested the Editor that it be printed on the front page. Why? Because a Senior once told me that she looked only at the headlines on the front page and threw the paper away since the rest of it was "just ads and stuff for and about kids."

Without the promise of enjoyment, it is hard to make Seniors venture into anything novel. So my piece in the newspaper and newsletter focused on encouragement—"come out and read something new"; on challenge—"get new ideas from what you discuss"; above all, on enjoyment—"meet new people, make new friends, have fun." This worked to the extent that Seniors were made aware of the program and were impressed (or amused) by the discovery that I had a doctorate. Some of them asked a few desultory questions about what I meant by New England poets. After which, most of them seemed to forget about it.

That was when I realized that I should not overlook a major issue in making any educational program viable for Seniors: the idea had to be **sold** to them, not just **told** to them, else I would be facing an empty room. Obviously I had to strategize further. So I requested the help of the Center's staff and they made sure to mention the new program casually, over coffee or lunch. Sometimes I stayed for lunch and then I talked to people at my table about the reason why I wanted to teach a course. (Each time I did this, I made sure to sit at a different table). It was good to get out of our houses or apartments, good to interact with others, wasn't it? If in the process we learnt something, wasn't that a plus too? I soon found that there were some Seniors who had a genuine interest in reading and so I coaxed them to help in publicizing the program. I spoke of it to other Seniors too—when I met them in the stores or in church or in friends' houses. Many of them did not consider themselves "Senior" enough to visit the Center, but they acknowledged that they were readers and hence interested in the course. And thus the news began to spread. But I still had roadblocks with the general Senior public.

My next hurdle was when I found that many were intimidated at the idea of reading, not light romances, not

Nora Roberts or Danielle Steel, but *literature*! One woman told me that she fell asleep when she tried to read Jane Austen, that she remembered her high school teacher telling the class to read Charles Dickens, but those books were so *long* and the language was so *difficult,* she could not think of going through all that again.

Here was another challenge. How to dissociate their minds from memories of mandatory school work and associate them with enjoyable reading? I asked a friend who had professed interest in the course for advice. She was an avid reader and looked forward enthusiastically to reading New England poetry. But, she told me, her high school teacher had insisted they learn parts of Longfellow's *Evangeline* "by heart," and that "put her off," so to speak. How would I go about overcoming that? We discussed the problem and decided that it should be stated at the outset (and repeated loud and clear!) that there would be no "homework," no tests or quizzes, nothing that could be called "mandatory." Over and over again, the word ENJOYMENT became a keyword for the course. She began to spread the word, and feedback became more positive.

Another "tentative" student, telling me *sotto voce* in the lunch-room that she was not sure if she should join because after all she was "just a high school graduate" with no college education at all, and perhaps she would find it… she hesitated…"above" her? Here was another challenge. Since most of the Seniors were NOT college graduates, possible feelings of diffidence or inferiority were strong reasons for many to keep out of any learning program. Why should she register for a class, asked the woman— softly, so as not to be overheard—when she did not know if she could complete it? Perhaps it would be a waste of money! Perhaps she would not understand a word! Perhaps she would not be able to sit for an hour in a classroom! She would love to learn something new but she did not know if she was smart enough…..?

Ah, the murky shadows of high school classrooms! How they hover over those who remember the grind without remembering the glory! Quickly I assured her that I was positive she *was* smart enough, that this would be very different to her memories of school: no memorizing, no tough questions that would be difficult to answer, and if she found it hard to sit for an hour, she could just excuse herself and leave the room. There would be no exams to study for, no papers to write, no tricky quiz at the end of a session—we would just get together and READ, DISCUSS, HAVE FUN. . I promised that we would choose books that were interesting stories, and would not be difficult to read. In the process, she would find that she had expanded her knowledge. She would find the class an occasion for socialization in an intellectual environment. Also, since she was so conscious of not having been to college, I told her that she would find out what a college level course is like without the constraints, practical problems and expense of actually attending a college. It would make her confident as well as give her enjoyment. And to cap it off, I said, there would be a pot-luck party at the end of the course! I guess I succeeded in convincing her, because she promised, rather nervously, to register for the program, and became one of the most interested students, faithfully joining course after course.

But after getting Seniors to register, it is possible for Centers to face two more hurdles: the physical location and the time of the class.

Location is very important. Some Centers are lucky enough to have classrooms complete with desks, chairs and boards. Some do not. Some teachers may have to cope not just with no classroom, but with the problem of no fixed room in which to meet. Sometimes participants may have to endure noisy surroundings, smells from the kitchen, uncomfortable chairs and no board, black or white. In this scenario, the Public Library is usually very ready to help out if space is needed. That way, teacher and students enjoy a comfortable room with air-conditioning/heating, board and markers, and chairs and tables, besides the peace and quiet that usually reigns in a library. Another important aspect of this venue is that it also promises enough parking for those Seniors who wanted to drive.

Timing is largely a matter of adjustment with the schedule of the Center since some Seniors who register may depend on the Seniors' bus for transport. That can be easily solved through organization. What is not so easily solved, and in fact, what can never be solved, is that Seniors sometimes have doctors' appointments that interfere with the scheduled class. If that happens, and it often does, the teacher can make a point of keeping handouts for those who are absent, and in the next class, rapidly re-capping what they missed. Re-capping, in fact, is appreciated even by those Seniors who are present, as it is a way of refreshing their minds with what went before.

When we finally started the project, I was pleasantly surprised to find that seven students had registered for this first experiment in Continuing Education. They were all eager, if slightly nervous. I did my best to be reassuring, to make my material absorbing, to encourage them to interact through discussion, to be punctual about stopping on time and to tell them at the end that they were doing "just great." Over the next few years my class expanded exponentially. Word of mouth worked wonders and signing up for a class became the thing to do for many Seniors in town. My hope was that students were joining the course because they were really interested. The whole purpose of the program was to have as many Seniors as possible involved.

And this brings me to the classroom material itself.

The course must be carefully planned. How would I approach the whole subject? How would I structure the material? What area of literature would I choose? How would I go about teaching it? To keep from developing a "frog-in-the-well" attitude, I could later choose material from other countries: for example, novelists from countries in the British Commonwealth. This would be a way of exposing Seniors to new cultures and experiences.

Thus was begun the program that now flourishes in our Senior community.

In this manner, other courses could also be formulated from other areas: History, Philosophy or Civilizations could be taught by other qualified volunteers. Perhaps among our town's Seniors there were other retired college professors willing to share their knowledge. Perhaps something would be served if at the end of the course Seniors learnt that people in the Middle East no longer traveled on camels, no longer lived in tents and actually had modern sanitation. Perhaps something would be served if at the end of the course they came out smiling and invigorated. And a great deal would be served when they registered for the next course, because it meant that their brains appreciated the stimulation provided by the material and by the people who attended it. We all know that contentment is worth more than a kingdom, and contentment should be the crown worn by Age. If learning something new brings contentment, for what more can any Director ask?

When about to retire from The New York Times, William Safire reminded readers that we can quit a job, but quitting "fresh involvement" is "mental peril." ("Engaging the Brain," The Dallas Morning News, January 25, 2005, p.11A). Never retire, he said in his article, but keep "your synapses snapping." The goal is to find Seniors to learn, but also Seniors to teach. Those with the qualifications to teach must be reminded that continuing to use our brains is like polishing a gem to make it shine better. It also lasts longer!

ii. ***The Icon and the Mouse:***

There are very few older people today who can look you in the eye and say "I teach my grand-children how to use a computer." It is usually the other way about. With a mixture of pride and humility (but mostly pride) they boast about the young ones in the family who type out their own assignments, browse the Web, play games, research their homework, or chat online with their friends. A recent study shows that 97% of teenagers use the Internet more than they watch television. Underlying the pride, indulgence and amusement older people feel at the technological expertise of children is a subconscious longing to equal them, even if only to know what it is that seems to glue them to a machine with such strength. Teaching Seniors how to use a computer and go online is a good way to prevent grandparents' irritation that instead of having fun with grandchildren, all they see is the children's backs as they sit hypnotized by that glowing screen in front of them. But once they learn how to use the Internet, irritation vanishes when the grandparents become as hypnotized as the kids. Now they can stay in touch with their grandchildren; and their self-esteem switches into an upward, instead of downward spiral.

A few organizations interested in advancing the technical competency of Seniors are researching ways and means of doing so. One such is CREATE or the Center for Research and Education on Aging and Technology Enhancement. With funds from the National Institute on Aging, they aim at researching how motor and cognitive skills are affected as people get older and have to cope with today's technology, even if it is only operating an ATM machine. But this had to be transformed into practical applications. Why should today's retirees wait for tomorrow's results? This is where our Senior Centers need to get their act together.

Most Centers today own at least one, if not many computers with Internet capabilities. Unfortunately they are not given optimum use; it is sad to see empty chairs in front of the machines. Perhaps it is because older folks are afraid that they will not be able to learn something new. Perhaps they are frightened of finding that they have lost certain skills, or never had them to begin with. There are Seniors who avoid computers as if the machines could jump up and bite them; Seniors who circle them hesitantly, but longingly, lacking the courage to ask for help and nervous that it would be beyond their capability; and Seniors—a microscopic minority—who sit confidently in front of them and play Bridge online. It is not true that older people cannot learn something new. This is a stereotype born of decades of negative thinking about aging and should be actively discouraged by people worth their salt who work in a Senior Center. Research studies have proved that they can. Encouraging a positive attitude is vital and with the right training, Seniors can learn twenty-first century skills. Proper guidance can work wonders for the memory, and using a computer implicitly encourages this kind of training; so every opportunity to do so must be given. In a matter of weeks they could be checking up on their investments, shopping online, emailing their family, or just dipping into the bountiful information that is available on the Web. No one has as much time as Seniors do. So why not put it to good use? The problem seems to be that most Seniors feel they don't "need" computers.

Take the case of an older women who would hover behind me as I sat typing; so one day I swung around and asked her if I could teach her how to use Word. "I can see that you are typing something," she told me, "but that's because you have something you want typed. What's the use of my learning whatever you call it? I'm not a novelist! And I write my letters by hand. So what is the point of learning?"

This is a valid argument. Seniors who are still employed usually know how to use Word or other programs because they *have* to. How to persuade someone who does not need Excel or Power Point or Word to learn them? And anyway, why should they?

This is where the Internet has made such a difference to Seniors. Only if older people are convinced that there is some reason for them to learn how to use a computer will they try to do so. I persuaded a man to sit with me at the computer, I logged into Google and gave him a demonstration of chatting on Google Groups. He was fascinated and finally convinced /that he should try and learn how to type, even if he did not have to learn to use Word. It took some coaxing, though. When I dangled the carrot of emailing his family, he retorted abruptly that he had no family with whom he would like to communicate. Carefully skirting that issue, I showed him how to sign up for a Group, how to chat with other Seniors about healthy eating or whatever took his fancy, and how interesting it was to gradually build up a feeling of "virtual" community that could replace that family he did not have or did not want. Sufficient to say that after a couple of months, he was one of the new students who became well and truly hooked on the Internet.

In the beginning, students have to learn the basics. First, they have to be taught the names associated with the machine. Even if some have used a computer before, it is important to start from scratch. Assume that the material is absolutely new, even if it is not new to some of the class. Remember that it is easy for an older person to be intimidated, and that simple language, a pleasant demeanor, and monumental patience are as necessary when teaching an 80 year old as much as when teaching anyone younger.

Talk about the computer: what does it consist of? Show them the monitor, the keyboard, the mouse, and the computer itself and explain that the work is done inside that tower that is usually placed under the desk. Let them write down the names of each part, or give them handouts. Even if it takes a little longer, my method is to make them write down the names themselves, since the very act of writing encourages the learning process. No matter if they are slow at writing—perhaps it is years since they took down notes. Remember not to overwhelm the student with information about the insides of a machine. It is unnecessary to teach how a computer works. After all, we use telephones with no idea of advances in fiber-optics or satellite communication.

It is important that students are not made to feel that they are in any way disadvantaged, so I make sure the text on the monitor is easily visible to those with low vision. Never ask Seniors if they have difficulty reading the font. Just assume that they would appreciate a larger font than normal. This could mean anything from a 14 point font to an 18 or even 20 point font. Eyesight can never be taken for granted in a Senior Center and rather than embarrass people by calling attention to poor vision it is more tactful to tailor the print to suit everyone.

Seat them in front of a computer, preferably just one or two people at a machine. Hands-on work is important and three people per computer would be neither practical nor interesting. Teaching Seniors to grip the mouse can be a challenge. Rather than make them feel clumsy, perhaps the use of keystroke commands instead of the mouse can be taught. (For example, show them that Control and P hit together brings up the Print screen instead of trying to make an unsteady hand use the mouse to hit File and then move it down to Print). Remember that trembling fingers can be embarrassing and so may prevent sensitive Seniors from tackling the computer at all.

Another important skill that a number of older people with unsteady hands find difficult is to use the scroll bar at the side of the screen. Parkinson's Disease or the mere process of aging can make fingers clumsy, hinder the focus and prevent the grip that is necessary to scroll up and down the screen. For the same reason it is hard to make them click inside a box in order to bring up the cursor but this will come with practice. If hands tremble, it is better to teach them the up and down arrow, or the Page Up and Page Down keys as an alternative, rather than make them feel incompetent and frustrated. Until that happy day when the human voice can activate the commands satisfactorily, Seniors will have to manage with the mouse or with keystrokes. Much of this depends on the student's own staying power.

I spent some time teaching one woman how to use keystrokes because her hand trembled so violently that it intimidated her. Discouraged and frustrated, she was ready to quit because of the way her hand slipped so that the arrow went wide of the scroll bar, of the down or up arrow, or sometimes across the whole screen. I kept a firm grip on my patience and showed her the keystrokes. But because her memory was not the best, I had to write them down on a piece of colored paper, hoping it would not get lost in the depths of the handbag she carried with her. I have the greatest admiration for this woman. Not only did she refuse to give up, she became (after a time) so skilled at the use of the Internet that I discovered her one afternoon playing bridge online. When I complimented her on acquiring such skills, she gave me a hasty glance, put her finger on her lip to shut me up, and went back to the game. I understood: she did not want her concentration disturbed. But I felt amply rewarded for the time I had spent teaching her.

Computer terminology takes time to learn. First it is wise to point out that words have changed their meaning. A "mouse" does not have four legs when it is part of a computer. Ask the student, "What is the desktop?" Explain why it is given that name. What is an "icon?" Talk about the difference between the traditional Eastern European religious image and the modern computer icon. Talk about the computer's "keyboard"—it is not a musical instrument. Most people have typed at some point in their lives, so it is easier to explain the keyboard than it is to explain the rest of the computer! If there are some who have not used a typewriter and have to search for the various keys, suggest that they get into the habit of using both hands on the keyboard rather than pecking out words with one finger.

Explain to them what a "program" is and that it has nothing to do with the theater, just as to "log on" has nothing to do with a cabin or a fireplace. Show them that a "window" is not something that needs drapes. Point out to them the "CD drive"—it has nothing to do with a bank. Perhaps you could put in a music CD and demonstrate how it works. In short, remember that these terms mean something else to an older generation than they do to youngsters today, and patiently explain their multiple meanings. And never talk down to Seniors. Remember that it is only Chance that has made the teacher more knowledgeable.

The previous material could be split into two classes, depending on time, the size of the class, and the number of available computers. Never rush a class. It takes time to process information as we get older and it is important to keep that in mind. Seniors should never feel that "it is too much to learn." They have all the time in the world, so why rush them? Repetition is helpful. At the next class, instead of immediately jumping into new material, give a brief recapitulation of what was done previously, just to refresh the students' memories.

Once the group is familiar with the computer as a machine, it is time to start simple programs. For those who have never typed before, familiarity with the keyboard is an important skill to be learnt. It is not hard to learn Word or

OpenOffice. First give them a book, fiction or nonfiction, and ask them to copy a page from it as practice. As they improve their keyboard skills they could move to letter writing and the use of tabs, dates and spacing. They could then graduate to copying a poem and the use of alignment, left, right or center.

It bears repeating to a teacher that words have changed their meaning: for example, note the meaning of the word "menu," something quite different to what they are accustomed. Teach them the various options on the menu beginning with File and Edit and the commands needed to Print. Just creating a file, editing it and printing it out is a huge step forward. "Cutting" and "pasting" need neither scissors nor glue but are useful in creating documents. The use of Format, Tools and Tables can be taught—*if need be*—much later. Never take it for granted that terms familiar to the teacher are as familiar to the student. I have found from experience that language has often bewildered Seniors and kept them from persisting with a computer class. For example, what is the meaning of "minimize" and "maximize" and how does one go about doing so? How does one "exit" a file?

Confidence is boosted by being able to see one's writing in print, by the ease in which erasing, moving, copying and pasting can be done—and confidence is all-important to a Senior, perhaps even more so than it is to anyone younger. Teach them to use Underline, Bold, or Italics. Show them how to Save As, to Save. This could easily take two to three classes. I repeat, DO NOT RUSH! As mentioned earlier, it is an acknowledged fact, and one that should be drilled into any teacher in a Senior Center, that as we get older we take longer to process information. Give them time to get comfortable with the machine and to learn what the machine does. As they progress, you could graduate to spreadsheets or Powerpoint for those who are interested. But initially, just learning to use a word-processing program is the most important skill that Seniors need to learn. Later when they use the Internet, these skills will prove advantageous. By some or all of the methods listed above, Seniors can familiarize themselves with computers. It must always be borne in mind that cognitive abilities expand as Seniors become familiar with technology. And now that the Internet has become a vast playing field in which they can disport themselves, the mental stimulation it brings has become an enormous bonus.

There is one important point that has to be remembered. Today's Seniors may be, for the most part, unfamiliar with computers and will need the training mentioned above. But this will not hold true ten or fifteen years from now. Baby boomers are not just familiar with computers; most of them have used them during their pre-retirement careers. In this case this chapter may not be as relevant for future Seniors as it is today, although here again there could be a minority who may benefit from it. Compared with today's Seniors, Baby Boomers have skills that could be utilized to hike the levels of mental and physical health. Actual material investments in Wall Street or real estate or whatever, should be turned into investments in one's own personal mental and physical health and sense of wellbeing through the use of available technology. It is vital that Director or instructor in a Senior Center thinks outside the box when it comes to planning for tomorrow's Seniors. Otherwise they might sniff in disdain at the old ways of doing things.

Which brings us to the Internet.

iii. *Keeping Up with Grand-children Online*:

Ask all Senior Citizens who are computer literate— they will tell you how easy it is now to keep in touch with grandchildren whether by email, chatting online through voice or text, or sending photos online. Some use the knowledge of technology not just to keep up with grandchildren's activities, but to give them advice or ideas, recommend books or just have fun. A certain Senior has a sister, another Senior Citizen, who lives 8000 miles away in another continent. She chats with her on Yahoo Messenger almost every day. Travel is no longer the enjoyment it once was, so why buy an expensive plane ticket, she asks, when they could talk to each other (and with a webcam, see each other)? Technology is the biggest boon to Seniors . It beats Bingo and movies any day because with a home computer, they sit in the comfort of their own houses and don't have to drive anywhere.

As previously mentioned, however, getting Seniors to go online can be an uphill task. Some nursing homes have installed computers with surprising results. It was discovered that residents were interested in using the web, even if only to communicate with their families. In Senior Centers, however, it is common to find resistance, especially because, unlike nursing homes, there are other alternative programs such as trips to places of interest and activities such as exercise, dance or art to keep people busy. Persuasion is only one method of overcoming resistance. Another way is to win them over by touting the exciting possibilities implicit in the Internet: not just emailing their families, but other conveniences like finding driving directions, shopping online, seeing pictures of their favorite plants, and so on. Information is available at one's fingertips apart from the fun of being connected to the rest of the world. This is especially important for Seniors who live alone. The internet can be a boon that turns loneliness into entertainment.

There is a multitude of websites for Seniors, and this has led to a new myth about them, as pernicious as the other negative myths. It is ironic that just as people assume that old age means decrepitude, those in charge of Senior programs now assume that it is enough to put information on the web and their duty is done. The paradox goes unnoticed. If older people are just sitting around waiting to push up the daisies, how are they to find the information that the government, for one, turns into electronic format? Isn't it ironical that Seniors cannot benefit from them because they are not computer literate? How are retirees to learn about the new Medicare law, about prescription benefits, about tax savings, unless they are first taught to access these sites? Firstgov.gov touches important topics like abuse of elders, fraud, consumer protection, elder rights, and so on. But how many Seniors read these web pages? Various organizations connected with Seniors happily key in mountains of information without stopping to ask "Can they read this information on the computer after getting used to seeing it in hard copy?" It is essential that every Senior, therefore, learns to use a computer, even if only for self-preservation.

According to the AARP there are at present more than forty million Seniors over the age of fifty who are online. I am inclined to keep an open mind on those figures, however. Different polls come up with different answers. Most seem to agree that not many over the age of sixty-five go online—perhaps around 25%. Those forty million obviously refers to younger Seniors. SeniorNet is a website that provides sites that could be of interest to Seniors, but more are needed, especially in what I call the "fun" category! Seniors have enough health problems and the means of learning more about them. What about giving them something to laugh about? Hopefully SeniorNet will come up with some interesting and recreational sites. This organization also conducts computer classes for a fee in different places, but there are not enough of them and not all are in Senior Centers. My focus is on Seniors who attend Senior Centers and have to be coaxed to go online.

Another way to win them over is to make the classes free of charge. Teachers are usually volunteers, so the Director's expenditure can be limited to whatever costs are incurred in order to get the machines up and running. In the Senior Center itself a signup sheet must be posted in a convenient place.

Once dates and times are agreed upon, the first class actually meets and students are now ready to begin. It is sometimes useful to circulate a few questions that will indicate just how much the class knows about computers. Have they ever used one? Have they ever used the Internet? However, even if one or two students know something about computers, it is always wise to begin as if they know nothing. Those who are quite unused to them should not feel left behind.

Begin the class with some background about the creation of the Internet. What is the Internet? How did it begin? Talk briefly about ARPANET. Who was responsible? How did it spread? Who was Tim Berners-Lee and what did he do in 1991 that made the Internet so accessible? I usually distribute a handout about the origin of the Internet so that the students can refer to it later and absorb it better. I also give them a handout about Charles Babbage, sometimes called the Father of the Computer, and Lord Byron's daughter Ada who, in the 1800s, combined her mathematical and imaginative skills to prophesy the future computer. Women always find this tidbit interesting. I tell them about the computer program named after her. I mention that the Internet is one of the greatest inventions after the invention of the printing press six hundred years ago. It has created the possibility of a "paperless" workplace. Explain why and how.

Now to the actual use of the Internet. Teach the students that they have to log on in order to access it, and explain that sometimes a user name and password may be necessary. What is a Server? Explain who the Server is and how it works. What is the difference between the Server and the Browser? What Browser is used by the Senior Center? Explain the different methods of getting connected—dial-up, DSL, cable, Wi-Fi. It might be useful to discuss the details of phone connections, local access numbers, etc. Once they have understood Servers and Browsers—and only hands-on use can make this clear—get down to specifics.

Start with a home page that they will be able to understand. Learning how to surf the Web is mainly a matter of practice. There is no need for Seniors to be taught details about FTPs, HTML, JPEG files and so on at this stage, though the teacher should be prepared for the occasional question. The main purpose of the class is not to learn the nuts and bolts of the Internet but how it can be applied to practical use. And I repeat what I said in the last chapter: information processing takes longer in older adults, so let them take their time to learn how the Internet works. Once they have mastered some of its capabilities, they will find that they have taken a big step forward. And once they get used to it they are not going to stop to bother about how it works. They will, in time, get used to the difference between the "virtual" and the "real" world of information. Teach them that this "virtual" world comes from millions of computers all over the globe that help us to access the information we need any time we need it, without having to run to a reference library. The power of the Internet is something they might want to think about.

Next introduce the students to searches. Show them the difference between a subject directory and a search engine. Teach them how to use Yahoo or Google to access various subjects such as maps and driving directions, games, phone numbers, etc. This could go on for the whole class since there is a lot to be absorbed. At the next class, show them the different capabilities of these search engines. Seniors are fascinated by the Images section, especially when they find pictures of their favorite plants and advice on the Web section about growing them. It is a boon to them when they discover that they can join Groups to chat on topics that interest them. Time must be spent on teaching how to join such groups. Advice must be given on maintaining their privacy and identity. Identity theft is spoken about so often by the media that it can be one of the reasons why Seniors are timid about getting on to the Web. So it is vital to calm their fears and show them how to maintain their privacy. Instructions on keeping their anonymity (emphasize that they should not type in any personal information) will be helpful and give them confidence.

Navigation buttons can be explained: the back, forward and refresh buttons, for example. Show them the address box and teach them how to go directly into a website by typing in the url, or uniform resource locator. Tell them that the url is like the address of a house and the Enter key is like a gate to enter the house.

Another class can be devoted to hyperlinks and how to use them. Show them what the pointing finger means, and the advantages of links. Show them how to read newspapers online, how to keep a list of Favorites, how to look at attachments and send attachments on their email. Bear in mind the fact that the utmost patience will be called for from the instructor. Some students may have trouble with their vision and I have known a few who change their glasses every few minutes, stand up to read the screen better, or demand help constantly because, as they cry indignantly, "my page has disappeared!" Keep your cool. Getting them to sit at a computer is the biggest hurdle, and once the teacher has cleared that, all that is required is the ability to be relaxed and helpful at the same time!

An important component of the class is evaluating a website and trying to determine just how authentic is its information. This is especially important to Seniors who search for health information on the web. Is the site relevant? Who has created the site and (most important) what are their credentials? When was the information put in—is there a date that can show us if it is outdated or current? Students should remember that the Internet does not always provide gospel truth and therefore they should keep their objectivity.

Finally, give them a list of websites that they might find interesting so that they may practice their search skills. They should learn to differentiate between the various domains. Teach them about the difference between the dot coms, govs, orgs, or mils. There are useful websites aimed at keeping the Senior community connected socially as well.

Apart from the online courses that they could join, they may find it exciting to feel that they are part of a global community. There are websites for Veterans, there are historical documents that might interest some, there are sites with health news and advice. In this context, I am careful to warn them about the possibility of unreliable advice on health matters. It is wiser to direct them to credible sites such as those provided by Medline, Mayo Clinic or the NIH. Retirees today are beginning to find that awareness about available resources can actually reduce their expenditure on doctors or on trips to the Emergency Room. A website such as merck.com with its online section on Health and Aging has information on various aspects of aging: its fundamentals, medical conditions, social issues, tips when undergoing surgery, caring for oneself, and so on, all of which are immensely useful to any Senior who knows how to use the Web. I have had students anxious to travel, but who want to look at the museums and art galleries online first so that they can decide where they want to spend time. Men love to look at the stock markets. Women tend to request sites that list crafts, recipes or gardening. The list of interesting websites seems endless!

Another advantage of being internet-savvy is that grandparents can keep in touch with grandchildren. Jane, for example, says she looks forward to her day because she knows her grandson's email will be waiting for her on her computer. It gave her a special feeling, she said, to know that he cared enough to write to her. Especially when there are grandchildren who do not live in the area and are perhaps met only once a year, the boon of being able to email or chat online cannot be over-rated. It can be one of the most heart-warming aspects of grandparenthood.

Then there is blogging. Is it just for the young, does anyone think? Absolutely not. Once Seniors are comfortable with going online it seems that there is nothing they cannot do. CNN's website reported that the new kids on the block are Senior Citizens caught in the blog mania. "Senior citizen bloggers defy stereotypes," says a CNN headline (Thursday, November 10, 2005). "Forget shuffleboard, needlepoint, and bingo. Web logs, more often the domain of alienated adolescents and middle-aged pundits, are gaining a foothold as a new leisure-time option for senior citizens." They cite statistics from the Pew Internet & American Life Project to show that 3% of seniors within the US have their own blogs and 17 percent have read someone else's blog. These figures are compared to the 18- to 29-year-olds of whom 13% have their own blogs while 32 % have read someone elses's blog. And the subjects cover a wide range. For example one ninety-two-year old farmer started a blog on tomato gardens that has been viewed more than 45,000 times. If one blogger misses his daily input, others email to ask if he/she is ill. This kind of virtual community that the Internet has created is a boon to lonely or isolated Seniors.

It is of primary importance then that the beginner is encouraged to gradually become relaxed and reassured when sitting in front of a computer. The instructor must remember that self-confidence in old age is a tender plant that needs nourishment. So a supportive teacher will be careful not to intimidate or confuse the student with too much information at a time. Confidence with use of the Internet encourages the can-do mentality that is so important as we age.

And this brings me to my final, very important reason for teaching Seniors how to go online. R U OK is the name given to certain programs, one being for teenagers and the other for Seniors. It is the latter that is relevant here. The way it works is that every morning a computer-generated phone call is made to the home of a Senior who lives alone. If the call is not answered, certain steps are set in motion to ensure that the Senior is "OK" and has not fallen or had a stroke or heart attack, or has succumbed to some illness and hence cannot pick up the phone. This is the kind of reassurance needed badly by children who worry about parents living alone, and by Seniors themselves who worry about falling and not being able to get help. But now that Instant Messaging is possible to anyone who has the Internet, technology has provided another kind of answer to this type of situation.

Take the case of a little old lady whom I shall call Doris. Her grandson took the trouble to teach her how to use Yahoo's email and then he initiated her into the mysteries of Yahoo Messenger and its Instant Messaging, with the little yellow smiley face that lights up when the user is online. Doris is delighted. She is not concerned about privacy issues, is thrilled that now she can make sure her son is at work and not taking another day off, that her grand-daughter is (hopefully) researching her homework.... Every morning she logs in, sees which of her family is online and sends them a chirpy one-liner. That way, she told me, she knows they are well. "I make sure I don't chat with them more than a minute," she assured me. "After all, I know they are busy with work. But it does make me feel good that they are doing OK and are not ill and that nothing has gone wrong." She does not quite realize that that is exactly what her family feels when they see that *she* is online.

Her son has a different take, of course. He told me that whenever he sees the yellow face near his mother's ID light up, he heaves a sigh of relief. "Thank God she is alive and well," he tells himself, "if she wasn't she sure would not be online!" Regina Chu points to the importance of family support when older adults decide to learn how to use computers. Once they have achieved proficiency, she asserts, great benefits from "e-learning" are to be garnered. An interesting point the writer makes is that women seem to benefit more from family support than men. Perhaps encouragement from children and grandchildren boosts self-esteem and validates the skills that seniors thought they had lost. By using "e-learning" they have proved to the family that the old lady still has a spark left in her!

There was the woman who faithfully IM-ed her sister who lived across the country. One day this sister died after a painful illness. She did not have the heart to delete her ID because as long as it was there it was as if her sister was still alive. A month later, she was astounded to see the little smiley face glowing against it. For a few seconds she gazed at it in disbelief. What was going on? Was the spirit world online too? Had her sister come back? Then a window popped up and a message came online: "Hi Aunty, did you think this was a message from the Other World?" she read, "It's just me, I'm using Mom's ID! Glad to see you online, guess you are OK!" Well, what a relief: it was her sister's daughter, not a technologically savvy ghost! Happily she proceeded to catch up with her niece's news.

My last recommendation to Seniors is to buy an Ipad. By the grace of God, Mr. Jobs and the magicians at Apple, Seniors now have a device that is ideal for them. The Ipad is a library packed into a device that looks like a slate. Here is the internet with all its capabilities, a shelf of books that can be read, a musical keyboard that can be played (even duets are possible), a bunch of games and puzzles, a dizzying number of applications (or "apps") and a radio. But what is most important for Seniors is that there is no need for shaky hands to cope with a mouse, the font can be enlarged to suit anyone's failing vision, and above all, the device can be held in the hand as Seniors relax in an armchair with their feet up on a table, thereby relaxing painful knees or swollen ankles. All one needs is a finger that will point to the surface to find material, turn a page or enlarge the font. What more can any Senior ask for? Of course, the Ipad is not cheap. But there are many who can afford to buy one (even if a Senior Center cannot) and hopefully prices will drop as time goes by.

iv. *Fly Me To the Moon—Singing with Sinatra.*

Surveys have shown what people have themselves demonstrated in the past: that if old folks had something creative with which to keep themselves occupied they would benefit mentally and physically. According to surveys, there were less falls, less medications, less depression and less loneliness when older adults were involved in doing something creative. Their self-esteem grew because they felt that their potential was being used. USA Today (06/17/2004) ran an article by Janet Kornblum—entitled "Arts help seniors age gracefully"—on this aspect of aging. The writer specifies one program where a group of seventy-five Seniors with an average age of eighty met once a week to sing under the guidance of a professional conductor. Age, it seems, has nothing to do with the desire to sing. I myself attended a concert at which a ninety-year old man sang a Christmas carol accompanied by his slightly younger wife at the piano. So why not organize regular weekly community singing groups in Senior Centers?

The renowned theologian Robert McAfee Brown

asks:

"How does one keep from "growing old inside"? Surely only in community. The only way to make friends with time is to stay friends with people.... Taking community seriously not only gives us the companionship we need, it also relieves us of the notion that we are indispensable."

The very act of standing together and singing is an exercise in the community spirit, a unifying experience, an act of togetherness. "I don't sing because I am happy;" said William James, "I'm happy because I sing." From my own experience of teaching singing to Senior Citizens, I have seen what rich rewards they reap.

First, just the simple act of getting out of their apartments, especially in winter, is a blessing to many of them. To those of us who are mobile, who have our own transport, who are busy with home or careers, it is not easy to imagine just how stultifying it can be to sit inside a house or apartment with nowhere to go, nothing to do and no one to talk to. Some old people have a favorite chair placed near a window so that they can catch any sign of life passing outside. Others watch birds, look at the plants outside, or just daydream. We do not need doctors to tell us that being sedentary is bad for the circulation, or that having nothing to occupy our minds can lead to depression. A program like community singing that involves getting older folk out of their abodes and into a comfortable, friendly, lively atmosphere has all to recommend it.

But there is more to community singing or singing in a choral group: it is good healthy exercise. To sing, one has to use one's lungs, and that is its second advantage. Seniors benefit hugely from the tips a teacher can give. Posture has to be taught because it is important to stand on both feet, back straight, head up. We sing not from our throats but more with breath from belly and lungs. Any yoga teacher can tell us the importance of deep breathing, just as any singing teacher can tell us the importance of breath control. In short, by exercising the lungs, singing improves not just our mental but also our physical health.

Then there is the interaction involved. The teacher may have her own list of songs but it is a good idea to ask the singers themselves for their ideas on what they would like to sing. Oh, how they enjoy singing the oldies—songs that reach back to their youth, to old boyfriends, to their bridegrooms, to their children… How often do they get misty-eyed when songs turn into nostalgic odes to the past! They remind each other---"do you remember this?" or "my husband loved that…" Even if it reminds them of loved ones gone, the fact that they *are* singing is itself a sign of resilience, of the necessity of "just going on." "Birds sing after a storm. Why shouldn't we?" asked Rose Kennedy. And so it is with many Seniors who have braved the storms of life and face a future that could be made more bearable by music. Some of those who come to join in the singing, sit around after the session is over and exchange stories, reminisce, or even execute little dance steps from long ago... In short, they are encouraged to "just go on!"

The mechanics of organizing a choir are the responsibility of the Director and the teacher. Transport must be made available for those who need rides. The room with the piano or keyboard must be free. And the teacher must be punctual and warming up at the piano so that when the singers enter, the tone is set and the atmosphere is right. It goes without saying that professionalism is not the goal. Enjoyment is. So there is no mention of auditions, of having any kind of previous experience, or of being able to read music. People are invited to join for the joy of singing not to excel as modern divas or Pavarottis. And there should be coffee and cookies for anyone who needs a break or a snack.

If by chance the teacher discovers that one in the group has no sense of music and does not sing in tune it would be tactful to ignore those false notes, no matter how they grate on other people's ears. This can be really hard but it is important not to put anyone down because they cannot sing in tune. The reason is the context. To overlook and forgive falsettos relates to the situation that brings them together to sing. Are these Seniors going to perform in theaters for the public? No. The main purpose in getting them together has already been spelt out: as long as they enjoy belting out a tune, as long as they try to give voice, far be it from the teacher (or any of the other singers) to be negative and pass discouraging remarks.

While the choice of songs is left very much to the teacher and the singers themselves, I have found that practicing with a purpose helps. For example, it would make sense for them to practice a list of Irish songs before St. Patrick's Day if there is the possibility of a party in the Center. Everyone knows "Danny Boy," "When Irish Eyes are Smiling," "Galway Bay," "Molly Malone" and such popular ditties, but a few may have to be taught "MacNamara's Band." (My singers enjoyed it so much that it turned into a marching band on the day of the St Patrick's party!

We also learnt groups of songs from different countries, and the kitchen provided popular dishes from that country for lunch to make it all more relevant. So we sang "Come Back to Sorrento," "Santa Lucia," "O Sole Mio" and such tuneful melodies that took care of Italy, while the group that had come for lunch ate pasta and other familiar Italian dishes. The day that our Director brought in a chef who demonstrated French cuisine, we sang "La Vie en Rose" in French. Everyone knows American patriotic songs that would make for a rousing concert on Flag Day. A few weeks can be devoted to Sinatra's popular oldies, always favored by Seniors. And of course after Thanksgiving the group devotes its practice sessions to Christmas Carols so as to be ready for the annual Christmas party. That is an occasion when the songs are copied and distributed to everyone attending the party so that all enjoy a glorious sing-along and the crowd goes home happy.

It makes sense to ask the singers to find a name for the group. There are quite a few such groups of Seniors who have given themselves symbolic names: the Golden Tones, the Silver Tones and the Twilighters are three I can remember. Choosing a name bestows dignity and an identity on the group and makes for greater commitment. They feel they "belong." Some even like to wear pretty tops bearing the name of their group. Others opt for a uniform-type dress or suit.

Finally, there is the very valuable therapeutic effect of singing.

It is an established fact that listening to music can soothe and in some cases even reduce symptoms such as blood pressure. What better reason than this for Seniors to involve themselves in listening and participating in some form of music? The New York Times reported a test that was conducted in a local hospital: one day, patients were astonished and intrigued to see a musician walking through wards playing the harp! They knew they had not yet reached the Golden Gates, so what was this about? Apparently the aim was to find out how music affected the sick in terms of blood pressure and other aspects illness. Results are still being evaluated and researched. Seniors may have to wait a long time for harps to become staples in their Centers, but the humble keyboard or its more sophisticated sister, the piano, is a good stand in. Some lucky Centers have guitarists too, who enjoy accompanying the songs.

Confidence is very important and this can be traced back to youth. People who grow up singing are never shy to begin again. Those who have been forced to sing in school or those who have been teased by friends or mocked by siblings are usually too timid to sing when they are older. When the questions "Would you like to join our chorus?" is put to them, the answer is often, "Oh no, I just can't carry a note." This may be true. Or it may not. Self-confidence is often hard to achieve. Lack of it may often be traced to negative comments made by some misguided singing instructor in school. Once they are coaxed into actually singing, however, a good deal of encouragement on the part of the teacher may be necessary to bolster budding interest. There is nothing like music to cheer the souls of Seniors and turn a dull evening into a happy one. The authors of *Senior Centers: opportunities for successful aging* also show the advantages of arts and creativity for an older population. (While I use a more guide-book type approach to learning, this is a useful if more theoretical book regarding Senior Centers). Senior Centers, therefore, could focus on starting choral groups without any of the demanding requirements on which more formal choruses insist. So let those voices be heard, let those lungs expand, let fun be the watchword!

   v.   *Keeping skills alive after retirement*
   There are many Seniors who need to keep on exercising the powerhouse that is the brain and so, they

keep on working instead of opting for retirement. Look at the number of public figures who are technically "Seniors" but are still busy with their careers: politicians, company directors, writers, Supreme Court judges. Cicero says it all: "So people who declare that there are no activities for old age are speaking beside the point. It is like saying that the pilot has nothing to do with sailing a ship because he leaves others to climb the masts and run along the gangways and work the pumps, while he himself sits quietly in the stern holding the rudder. He may not be doing what the younger men are doing, but his contribution is much more significant and valuable than theirs. Great deeds are not done by strength or speed of physique: they are the products of thought, and character, and judgment. And far from diminishing, such qualities actually increase with age." (Cicero, 220)

Cicero also quotes a number of Greek and Roman writers who remained "actively at work" till they died. He cites Sophocles who kept writing his famous tragedies into old age. In fact, his sons thought he was neglecting the family property and so they took him to court. But when he read from the play he was writing, Oedipus in Colonus, the magistrates were so impressed that they dismissed the case. His writing, they said, showed no signs of a weak mind.

At some point, however, people do decide to retire. Even if they do, why should they put their skills to sleep just because they are no longer following their careers? Why should teachers, for example, stop teaching just because they are (technically) retired? Could they not turn their teaching expertise to good use after retirement? Seniors with the necessary qualifications could involve themselves in some kind of educational program that would benefit themselves as well as other Seniors. It would encourage them to keep their balance on the wire of mental stimulation and keep them *thinking*.

Just as there are subjects that will interest Seniors who want to learn, there are subjects that will interest Seniors who are capable of teaching. It could be anything ranging from astronomy to architecture. One of the questions raised in a class may be about the credentials of the teacher, Copies of resumés could be kept available to anyone interested. Students need assurance. If they have no confidence in the instructor, interest will flag.

There are other angles that have to be kept in mind. Obviously, the teacher must know the subject very well. There is no point in trying to teach in a slip-shod manner, thinking that these are after all "only Seniors." Research and preparation are obligatory. Seniors are not children. They have a lifetime's experience in perceiving who is genuine and who is flaky. Studying the subject and being prepared for all kinds of questions increases the teacher's self-confidence, and that confidence affects the group being taught. They have to trust the teacher and approve of his/her expertise.

Next, technique is vital. No matter how clever a teacher, if a presentation is boring, the class is lost and will soon diminish in size as people drop out. The teacher's voice should be light and friendly, not patronizing or declamatory, not too loud, not too soft and certainly not a monotone. There should be no talking down to the listeners. A friendly conversational tone is preferable to the authoritarian tone that lecturers sometimes use with teenagers. Interest, interaction and input are the three I's that the teacher should never forget. Most important at the very beginning is to set the parameters of the class. The aim being *Enjoyment*, there would be no exams to study for, no papers to write, no quizzes to prepare for, in short, there would be no pressure. The only requirement would be the willingness to listen, read and to talk about what was read. Discussion and questions would be encouraged, and the three I's were the sole guiding factors in the conduct of the course. The Seniors in the class should feel comfortable— and not just physically. They should feel that this was a place to learn something with the least possible stress.

On the first day, Seniors will trickle in, some looking shy and embarrassed, some confident and eager. A few may know each other, others may not. In a very light and casual tone they could be welcomed, the enjoyment factor stressed and the fact mentioned that education does not always depend on a college degree but more on the will to learn something new. Since most of them may not have any college education, this immediately makes them feel less embarrassed and more confident. The aim is to make them feel as comfortable psychologically as they are physically. It is hard for teachers of young people to realize how intimidated Seniors can feel in a classroom setting. Remember that for most of them it could be fifty years (or more) since they graduated from high school. Sitting in a classroom is a new experience. (And it IS a classroom. Chairs are arranged formally, there is a board, the teacher has his or her own desk and chair. Some might prefer tables around which people may sit, but that is a matter of convenience and availability).

There is always room for thinking, whether the class focuses on art, history, astronomy or whatever. Ideas should be expressed in simple but not simplistic language. These are Seniors who have lived long lives, who have experienced many of the joys and sorrows that form the basis of literary themes, who have weathered storms that in some cases are more traumatic than those created by a novelist. Instead of pointing to future possibilities, as one does with college students, the teacher often has to remember that Seniors are looking at the past, both as paradigm and remembrance. Reflections inspired by whatever material is being taught can easily be turned by them not just into theory but into its exemplification in their own lives. The teacher of a Senior Citizens class has to be something of a Janus, therefore, looking forward for some and backward for others. When Seniors begin to discuss such issues (and they must always be linked to the text) the sharing of thoughts becomes both diving-board and pool for debate. And such debate can often be truth-seeking in nature, even if the Seniors would never think of it in such terms.

Writing down their thoughts could be encouraged. While *discussion* of the past is salutary, describing it on paper is even better. For example, students might like to talk about growing up during World War II. But what about pinning them down to *write* about specific happenings in their lives during that period? One woman told us about her experience as an auxiliary in the Navy. Another had wonderful tales to tell about factory life and working as a real Rosie the Riveter. It is hard to find an older person who has not had some experience that he or she could turn into an autobiography. There may have been joyful events, tragic occurrences, catastrophes or adventures that would make for interest. Putting these experiences into writing is not as easy as verbal nostalgia. A good teacher may be able to inspire some of them, if not all, to attempt to write them down, not just talk about them. In this way, writing skills can be developed. Students may be shown how to brainstorm, how to outline, how to expand ideas, and the actual writing could be done either at home or in class. Most important is the fact that this is one way of activating memory, of burrowing into the past to unearth happenings that they thought they had forgotten about, or of just keeping the mind busy and interested.

Another advantage of writing life stories is that it is invaluable therapy where mental health is concerned. Just putting down on paper the emotions felt at some tragedy or disaster in each one's life is a means of coming to terms with it. Feelings of grief and of loss after the death of a spouse can be helped, if not completely assuaged, by writing. The act of putting pen to paper could be a means of fighting depression and of boosting self-esteem. If they are sensitive about reading out their work in class, never make it an issue. Their need for privacy must be respected.

Finally, writing about one's earlier life is an excellent stimulus for learning how to organize thoughts and then putting those thoughts into actual sentences. It helps to put the past into perspective by cutting things down to size, by realizing how things have changed and perhaps improved. It is something like an inner cleansing, what is called "purgation" in Greek tragedy. It is also a way of memorializing their lives for their grandchildren, of telling them about the culture in which their parents and grandparents grew up. All in all, objectifying and recording experience contributes to mental energy and is one of the healthiest of activities for Seniors. A good instructor will be able to make his/her students comfortable, instead of intimidated, as they explore their past.

Conclusion: Destroy the Myth or Perish with It

The preceding pages are meant to be suggestions and guidelines—nothing more. Any Director worth the name will have his or her own ideas about how to expand the Senior Center's activities. Any teacher worth the name will have his or her own ideas on how to engage Senior Citizens in creative activities, whether technological, literary or artistic. The primary goal is to keep Seniors interested and mentally involved. How often I have found someone prostrated by grief over the death of a lifetime friend or a spouse. How grateful they are when I persuade them to join my literature class. "It takes my mind off my worries," is a common reaction. "It gives me something else to think about." There are many other avenues that could serve the same purpose. And the purpose is to improve their quality of life.

English as a Second Language is one such and it would be especially popular in Centers where there are many immigrants. Parents who have accompanied their children to this new country suffer alienation and isolation because they cannot communicate with the neighbors or with salespeople in the stores. A great deal of misery, loneliness and depression would be remedied if only they could be persuaded to attend classes in a Senior Center. It would help integrate them into the community and thus be of huge psychological benefit. It would also be a positive step in giving them more opportunities, perhaps for employment and certainly for enjoyment. This is an issue that bears examination and research. Not much attention is paid to Seniors who belong to ethnic minorities and who do not speak English. The quality of their lives too would be augmented with the ability to just *communicate* with the neighborhood instead of their having to depend on children or grandchildren to function as interpreters.

Senior Centers in cities could undertake such projects and may easily find the funding for them. There is a demand for teachers of English in East Asian communities in Dallas, and the demand too, for expansion of such services among Hispanics. Why should only young immigrants be given these opportunities? The aged are every bit as needy, perhaps more so, because not knowing how to speak in English can result in isolation and the depression that often accompanies old age. It is necessary for lonely Seniors to bond with people in a new country. In fact, such a step would be of immense value in improving race relations. Communication can wipe out barriers and prejudices that are based on ignorance of other life styles. The need to speak English does not have to be always linked to or gauged by its commercial value—by which I mean that learning English need not be linked only to getting a job. It is of vital sociological and psychological importance to those who never had one.

Senior Centers can play a huge role in this context. Consider the inter-cultural programs that could be started: Directors must remember that immigrants who have learned to speak some English may bring valuable contributions to programming. For example, some could demonstrate the crafts popular in the countries from which they came, others could give cooking demonstrations. But the knowledge of English is mandatory for such programs to succeed in our Senior Centers.

Apart from English as a Second Language, art classes are conducted in many Centers and prove very popular. Art appreciation can be linked to visits to local art museums. Quilting is popular with a number of women and wood-carving appeals both to women and men. And what about theater groups? Seniors could get together to perform one-act plays. Just as confidence is needed to get people to sing, confidence is needed to get people to act. But it is not impossible. Memorizing lines increases brainpower and those who have acted in their youth might be happy to get back onto the boards again. If they do not want to actually act, just sitting comfortably on chairs and reading out the parts (what is called "play-reading") is an education to those who read and to those who listen.

Finally, Directors of Senior Centers would do well to remember that the time is fast fading away when all that they had to organize were blood pressure clinics or Medicare seminars. Baby Boomers, our new Seniors, will be happy to attend them; but they will also demand something more challenging and interesting than just sitting back, focusing on their health problems and Waiting for God. If they do not find what they want, it might just happen that Senior Centers will face a diminishing population. Why? Because other organizations will surely step into the breach and think up programs and projects that will keep Baby Boomers mentally healthy and physically active. Soon commercial organizations will realize that there is a vast untapped pool of profit that can be garnered from the Boomer demographic strata. Community colleges are trying to step into the breach and this is a positive development. But their resources may stretch only to organizing a few courses for Seniors. Non-traditional locations might fill the gap. Perhaps church basements or even restaurants may provide necessary locations for Elder learning.

This is what Directors of Senior Centers must bear in mind: that to validate their existence they should contribute to the educational as well as the physical needs of their future members and encourage them with enriching, interesting, intellect-stimulating programs. As the French writer Andre Maurois said: "Old age is far more than white hair, wrinkles, the feeling that it is too late and the game finished, that the stage belongs to the rising generations. The true evil is not the weakening of the body, but the indifference of the soul." Or perhaps it can be traced to the indifference of the Director.

It is this indifference that has to be vanquished in the decades to come for the various Councils on Aging to continue to be vital in society. In the macro context, it will also be a benefit to the nation. If indifference is not overcome, Senior Centers may perish without new and interesting programs that justify their existence.

Educating the public is important too. The advantages of organizing Continuing Education programs for Seniors must be touted in the media. Surely it is time state and federal agencies put money and manpower into them. Considering the benefits to mental and physical health it is of prime importance that Directors involve themselves in seeking aid for such programs. Politics should not stand in the way of reorganizing budgets and thinking outside the box. A Director worth his or her salt will realize that money spent on education may in the long run be instrumental in reducing the number of clinics and nurses' visits to Centers. For when more and more Seniors achieve healthy minds and bodies, why would they need constant doctoring? The myth that old people need only physical care and nothing else is fast dying out. If in some places this myth is perpetuated by concentrating only on such care, it needs to be destroyed by turning to alternatives.

We have seen that according to reliable medical opinion, brainpower can be increased with the stimulus of learning something new. It bears repeating that hidden benefits result when Seniors keep mentally healthy because, in the larger context, this is good for the nation. To encompass this aim, continuing education must be made possible and in a democracy it should be made available to anyone in society, not just the elite who can afford to pay for it in colleges. Various courses have been suggested as guidelines to interested Directors of Senior Centers and future instructors, though these are just guidelines, not mandates. Instructors will come up with new ideas and methods of putting them into execution. As long as there is interest, there will be rewards.

But for how long? Realism impels us to consider how much time Seniors have left to them. In an age of expanding technology and healthcare, years are being added to the average age at which old people die today. They did not live as long in those days before health care improved and social security provided the safety net of financial resources and independence. The flip side of new longevity is that loneliness and isolation from families have been a result. The euphoria that accompanied the established of Sun City and other retirement communities like it has diminished somewhat. Golf and the frenetic enjoyment of leisure cannot replace the support and community from family connections. Isn't it vital then that these years be spent in engagement with the world, not in isolation from it, in continuing interest in what is going on, not in ignorance of current thinking?

The spirit of volunteerism that inspires the teachers and the taught only increases their quality of life. How complete would life be if, at its end, we know the tranquil joy of having dealt with age in the best possible way! How grateful our families would feel if they knew that their loved one had benefited from the kind of interaction that did not involve only wheelchairs or RNs but included the learning and doing, that spelt fulfillment. This is what Continuing Education can do. Then when that last hour strikes, when that curtain falls in a final adieu, how much more beautiful would that passing be to everyone in the family because it has been a life well spent and fully enjoyed.

BIBLIOGRAPHY:

Anderson, Norman B. *Emotional Longevity. What really determines how long you live._*NY: Viking Penguin, 2003.

Begley, Sharon. "Even Old Brains seem Flexible enough to Enjoy a Workout." Science Journal, *Wall Street Journal*, Friday December 2, 2005.

Beisgen, Beverly A. and Kraitchman, Marilyn Crouch. *Senior Centers: opportunities for successful aging.* N.Y. Springer Publishing Co. 2003.

Chu, Regina Ju-Chun. "How family support and internet self-efficacy influence the effects of e-learning among higher aged adults--Analyses of gender and age differences. " *Computers & Education.* 55. 1 (August 2010): 255 (10).

Cicero. *Selected Works.* Tr. Michael Grant, Penguin Classics, 1960; rpt. 1971.

Cohen, Gene D. *The Creative Age: Awakening Human Potential in the Second Half of Life.* NY: Avon Books, 2000.

Dychtwald, Ken. *Age Power. How the 21st Century will be ruled by the New Old.* NY: Tarcher/Putnam Books, 1999.

Eberstadt, Nicholas. "Old Age Tsunami," *wsj.com*, November 15, 2005.

Freedman, Marc. *Prime Time: How Baby Boomers will Revolutionize Retirement and Transform America.* PublicAffairs Press: 1999.

Kornblum, Janet. "Arts help Seniors age gracefully." *USA Today*, 06/17/2004.

Lamdin, Lois and Fugate, Mary. *Elderlearning: New Frontier in an Aging Society.* Phoenix, AZ: Oryx Press, 1997.

Lowy, Louis. *Why Education in the Later Years?* D.C. Heath and Co., 1886.

Minois, Georges. *History of Old Age: From Antiquity to the Renaissance.* (1987). Tr. Sarah Hanbury Tenison. University of Chicago Press, 1989.

Morris, Virginia. *How to Care for Aging Parents.* NY: Workman Publishing Company, 1996, 2004.

Pardasani, Manoj. "Senior Centers: increasing minority participation through Diversification." *Journal of Gerontological Social Work.* 2004, Vol 43, Issue 2/3, pp.41-56.

Perls, Thomas and Silver, Margery Hutter. *Living to 100.* Basic Books, 1999.

American Council on Education. "Report suggests ways to strengthen educational opportunities for older adults."

On Campus with Women_ 38.2 (Fall 2010): NA. *Academic OneFile*. Gale. 19 July 2010),

Roizen, Michael F. *RealAge: Are you as young as you can be?*. HarperCollins 1999.

Rowe, John W and Kahn, Robert L. *Successful Aging.* NY: Random House, 1998.

Schneider, Edward L. *AgeLess: Take Control of your Age and stay Youthful for Life_.* NY: St. Martin's Press, 2003.

Shakespeare_ *The Comedy of Errors.* II. ii. 47, 48.
"Was there ever any man thus beaten out of season,
When in the why and the wherefore is neither
rhyme nor reason?"

Snowden, David. *Aging with Grace: What the Nun Study teaches us about leading Longer Healthier and More Meaningful Lives.* NY: Bantam Books, 2001.

Springer, Mellanie . et al. "The Relation Between Brain Activity During Memory Tasks and Years of Education in Young and Older adults," (*Neuropsychology*, 2005, Vol. 19, No. 2).

Trafford, Abigail. *My Time: Making the most of the rest of your life.* Basic Books, 2004.

Vaillant, George E. *Aging Well.* Little, Brown and Company, 2002.

Victoroff, Jeff. *Saving Your Brain.* Bantam Books, 2002.

Weaver, Frances. *The Girls with the Grandmother Faces: A Celebration of Life's Potential for those over 55.*
 NY: Hyperion, 1996.

Williams, Janice Lake and Downs, Janet. *Educational activity programs for Older Adults.* NY: Haworth Press, 1984.

Yenerall, Joseph D. "Educating an Aging Society: The University of the Third Age in Finland." *Educational Gerontology*, September 2003, Vol. 29, Issue 8, p.703.

. . . .

Made in the USA
Lexington, KY
10 January 2011